EUROPA ⚔ MILITARIA
SPECIAL N°10

NAPOLEON'S LINE CAVALRY

RECREATED IN
COLOUR PHOTOGRAPHS

STEPHEN E. MAUGHAN

Windrow & Greene

Dedication:
To the shades of Edward, William and Star

This edition published
in Great Britain 1997 by
Windrow & Greene Ltd
5 Gerrard Street
London W1V 7LJ

Designed by John Anastasio/Creative Line
Printed in Hong Kong through Bookbuilders Ltd

A CIP catalogue record for this book is
available from the British Library

ISBN 1 85915 038 1

Author's note:
The photographs in this book were taken at events
around Europe over four seasons, and represent the
recreated French Cavalry in all its aspects as it
may currently be seen on the European re-enactment
circuit. Rarely were more than one or two cavalry
groups present at any one event, with the exception
of Waterloo, which attracts units like no other
re-enactment. By the time the photography for this
book and its companion volumes on Napoleon's Line
Infantry & Artillery and Napoleon's Imperial Guard
was complete, almost ten thousand miles had been
travelled and almost three thousand photographs
had been taken. The Emperor, it seems, is still a
man to be followed...
   A limited edition print run (10ins. x 8ins.) of
each of the photographs in this book is available
from: Five Star Photography, 34 North Lodge Terrace,
Darlington, Co.Durham DL3 6LY, England - prices on
application.

Acknowledgements:
My deepest thanks go to my wife Alison, not only for
typing and correcting the manuscript but also for
being herself and being there whenever I have needed
her. I also wish to express my gratitude to all of the
re-enactment groups who have taken part in the
photographic sessions which made this book possible.
The contact addresses, at the time of writing, of these
and other groups currently re-creating French Napoleonic
cavalry were as above right:

In Great Britain:

1er Chasseurs à Cheval, Centre & Élite Companies
(members of the Napoleonic Association):
Hamish McCloud, 82 Beresford Road, North End,
Portsmouth, Hampshire PO2 0NQ; Mike Grove, Upper
Wood House Farm, Holmbridge, W.Yorks HD7 1QR

1er Lanciers de la Garde (Polish Lancers)
George Lubonski, 10 Skipton Road, Silsden BD20 9JZ

Grenadiers à Cheval de la Garde
Morris Boakes, 12 Cranfield Road, Aylestone LE2 8QQ

In France:

5eme & 7eme Hussards (Centre Companies)
Hussards de Lasalle, c/o Jean-Pierre Mir,
7 Impasse de Balmes, 78450 Villepreux

Compagnie d'Élite, 7eme Hussards
William Cagnard, 51 Rue Sedaine, 75011 Paris

Chasseurs à Cheval de la Garde
Joel Dupas, 70 Rue Osselet, 59247 Fechain

In Holland:

14eme Cuirassiers
Paul Deideren, Willem II Singel 52,
6041 HT Roermund

2eme Lanciers de la Garde (Red Lancers)
Robert Marcus, Elandstraat 16, 2513 ER Den Haag

In Belgium:

2eme Dragons
Gerard Bourlier, Chemin de St Germain 7,
1420 Braine l'Alleud

In Italy:

5eme Cuirassiers
Roberto Tortonese, Chiappero, via Olevane 93/A,
Grugliasco, Torino

Introduction

Following his *coup d'état* of 18 Brumaire (9 November 1799) the armies of the French Revolution passed entirely under the command of former General, now First Consul, Napoleon Bonaparte. The cavalry arm which he inherited comprised 85 regiments: 25 of Chasseurs à Cheval, 13 of Hussars, 20 of Dragoons, two of Carabiniers and 25 of Cavalerie de Bataille (heavy cavalry). During the Revolutionary Wars the French cavalry had earned an inferior reputation, making a poor showing against their Austrian and Prussian adversaries; a regional Inspector-General of Cavalry reported:

"The mounted regiments are in a deplorable state. The great familiarity which exists between superiors and subordinates, and the crass ignorance of senior officers - who, scarcely knowing how to sign their names, cannot read let alone understand the military regulations which they should be applying - has utterly destroyed discipline. I have seen regiments deficient in everything, whose horses have not been groomed for a year because there are no implements with which to do it. The cavalry which France possesses at this moment is useless."

The battles of the Revolutionary Wars had been fought largely by hastily trained and equipped recruits formed into massed infantry units around an armature of veteran pre-Revolutionary regulars, following a deliberately simplified tactical doctrine. Meeting the greater and more specialised demands of an effective cavalry arm had been beyond France's resources; most units were under-manned and under-mounted, and dispersed among the infantry in wasteful "penny packets". Napoleon believed in concentration of force, and from the time of his first independent command in Italy he had stripped the mounted regiments away from the infantry divisions and grouped them into independent brigades under younger and more able leaders.

The task which faced the First Consul and his new breed of cavalry commanders in 1799 was formidable; and the improvement achieved was extraordinary - as early as June 1800 Kellermann's cavalry played a major part in the victorious counterattack against the Austrians at Marengo. The French squadrons acquitted themselves well against the combined might of Austria and Russia in the 1805 Austerlitz campaign; and in the Jena/Auerstaedt campaign the following autumn they outfought the much-vaunted but now neglected and ill-led Prussian cavalry, culminating in one of the most dramatic pursuits in history. Murat's charge at the head of 80 squadrons - nearly 11,000 riders - at a crisis of the battle of Eylau in February 1807 saved the day: it advanced 2,500 yards, smashed through the Russian centre, cut down their artillery crews, and withdrew for a loss of 1,500 men.

By the Wagram campaign of 1809 adequate remounts and troopers of the old calibre were becoming more difficult to find. A huge effort was made to assemble and mount the multinational army which Napoleon led into Russia in June

1812; but the disastrous campaign which followed saw the virtual destruction of the Emperor's cavalry - of the 176,850 horses recorded as taken into Russia, only some 1,500 remained with the army at the end of the year. While the Emperor succeeded in raising more than 200,000 new troops by April 1813, he was unable to compensate for the loss of horseflesh and trained cavalrymen, thus fatally compromising his campaigns of 1813-14 and leading directly to his downfall and first abdication. The heroic but ultimately vain efforts of Napoleon's cavalry at Waterloo in 1815 are the stuff of legend.

That re-enactors should seek to recreate the gorgeously-uniformed troopers of Napoleon's army is unsurprising; that the groups of private individuals featured in this book should have succeeded in doing so to the standards illustrated here is remarkable. The financial expense, organisation, logistics, dedicated hard work and level of special skills demanded by cavalry re-enactment are all much greater than those required of the foot-soldier. Above all, a horse is still a horse: it must be fed, watered, groomed, and exercised; its stable or piquet line must be kept clean, and its wellbeing must always come first. It is as true of today's re-enactor as it was of the Napoleonic soldier that:

"It is of the greatest importance that the recruit should learn from the very beginning to look upon his horse as his best friend, and not as a source of trouble and annoyance to him. It must be impressed upon him that without his horse he is useless, and that he must spare no trouble in maintaining its efficiency and welfare."

3

Chasseurs à Cheval

The Chasseurs à Cheval (lit."hunters on horseback") were the most numerous branch of Napoleon's light cavalry. At its peak this category would comprise regiments numbered from 1 to 31 (the numbers 17 and 18 were vacant; and the 30eme Chasseurs were converted to form the 9eme Chevau-Légers Lanciers).

The Chasseurs were the original French light cavalry arm, and traditionally wore dark green uniforms - indicative of their light status - faced with regimental identifying colours. Tactically they were intended to perform the same role as the Hussars: reconnaissance, screening, raiding, and pursuit of a beaten enemy (yet most light cavalrymen still carried in their hearts the desire to crash home in a full-blooded charge, scattering the foe before them).

French Revolutionary cavalry were notorious for their lack of discipline and their inability to perform the manoeuvres laid down in the 1788 Cavalry Training Manual, and they needed firm handling to bring out the best in them. One of the most informative of cavalry memoirists, Marcellin de Marbot, was posted to the Bercheny Hussars (later the 1st Hussars) during this period; and his portrait of a light cavalryman of the old school - Sergeant Pertelay - is probably typical:

"...A jolly ruffian, very well set up I must admit, with his shako over his ear, his sabre trailing, his florid countenance divided by an enormous scar, moustache half a foot long waxed and turned up to his ears, at his temples two long locks of plaited hair which came from under his shako and hung to his breast - and withal, such an air!"

Chasseur regiments were composed of between four and six squadrons each commanded by an *adjutant* (major). Each squadron comprised two companies, commanded by *capitaines;* and each company was made up of two troops or *pelotons,* commanded by *lieutenants* or *sous-lieutenants.* The strength of a cavalry squadron - though full establishment was a rare occurence when in the field - was about 135 officers and men. The company was supposed to field one *capitaine,* one *lieutenant,* two *sous-lieutenants,* one *maréchal-des-logis-chef* (sergeant-major), two *maréchaux-des-logis* (sergeants), one *brigadier-fourrier* (quartermaster-corporal), four *brigadiers* (corporals), one trumpeter and 54 troopers.

(Above & opposite) The Chasseur in our photographs wears a combination of uniform items typical of the early 1790s. The fur-crested "Tarleton"-style leather helmet was replaced from 1795 by a *mirliton* cap. Note the cheap printed fabric imitation leopardskin turban; and the plume in a mixture of green and red - apparently the most popular of a number of colour combinations seen. The fashion was still for long hair, dressed in a central rear queue and two braids from the temples. When young Marbot joined the Bercheny Hussars he was sold a false queue and sidelocks by the regimental barber; his sergeant painted a moustache on his face with blacking. (Bonaparte's preference for short, hygienic hair styles cost most of the cavalry their tresses, but there were exceptions: the 15th and 26th Chasseurs kept their hair long until at least 1813.)

The *dolman* jacket in dark green, worn here with a braided waistcoat and riding overalls, had three rows of pewter buttons and 13 to 18 rows of white "lace" on the breast. The dolman was not manufactured under the Empire, and was increasingly replaced by the *habit-long* - a plain green long-tailed coat with turned-back lapels - for everyday uniform; but many regiments hoarded their dolmans for years afterwards, at least for full dress, and a surviving dolman of the 4th Chasseurs is stamped 1808.

The scarlet collar and cuffs here identify the 1st Chasseurs (who still wore the dolman on campaign at least until 1806). Each group of three numbered regiments was identified by a colour: scarlet for the 1st, 2nd and 3rd Chasseurs, bright yellow for the 4th, 5th and 6th, and thereafter in order rose, crimson, orange, sky blue, *aurore* (peach), *capucine* (nasturtium), madder red, *amarante* (maroon), and *chamois* (buff). Within each group the first regiment had both collar and cuffs in facing colour, the second cuffs only, the third collar only.

Aymar de Gonneville leaves us a description of the 20th Chasseurs of this period: "...Robin was a regular brigand and looked like one; he had committed pillage, rape, murder, and this was known to the whole regiment. The rest of the company was well supplied with men of this stamp, and the horrible stories they told in the barrackroom of an evening made ones hair stand on end. But among them were also to be found admirable instances of bravery, of which they boasted much less than their misdeeds."

5

(Right & opposite)
A trooper of the 1st Chasseurs in about 1808. In that year the *habit-long,* by then generally worn for all orders of dress, began to be replaced by this short-tailed, single-breasted *Kinski* jacket, piped and faced in the same sequence of identifying colours as the dolman, with short turned-back tails and shoulder straps with three-pointed outer ends. As was usually the case with all Napoleonic uniforms, however, there was considerable diversity in practice; old garments were kept in use until they wore out, and unit and personal preferences ensured that there was a good deal of variety between regiments and squadrons, and even within single companies. The sleeveless waistcoat continued to be a popular choice for such variation: officially white in summer, dark green in winter, it was often seen in regimental colours, decoratively cut and braided.

The plain 1806 shako has here replaced the mirliton and the fancy 1801 shako which retained the mirliton's *flamme* - a long triangular streamer of coloured cloth usually worn wrapped around the shako body. The introduction of the 1806 model's metal-scaled chinstraps made the cap cord purely decorative; on previous types of headgear it had been carried down to loop round or button to the torso to prevent the cap being lost in action.

In contrast to the simple knucklebow hilt of the sidearm reproduced on page 4, our trooper of c.1808 carries the three-bar-hilted Year XI model light cavalry sabre, which had an iron scabbard. Some earlier models had leather and brass alloy scabbards which were prone to bending out of shape, sometimes jamming the weapon; sabres and scabbards were always vulnerable to damage due to wear-and-tear in the field. General Gassendi recorded that the introduction of the iron scabbard ended complaints about bending; now his men complained about the increased weight...

(Left) Trooper of the 1st Chasseurs practices giving point, as described in the period drill manuals. The main French school of thought advocated the thrust with the point of the sabre rather than the cut with the edge; General de Brack, author of *Avant-postes de Cavalerie Légère,* suggested that the cut be used only as a backhand stroke against an opponent who had already ridden past. The British 1796 cavalry manual by Le Marchant placed emphasis on the cut; but the argument over the relative merits of the cut and the thrust had raged among cavalrymen for centuries. (Frederick the Great had remarked: "Kill your enemy with either one or the other - I will never call you to account for which you used.")

The French memoirist Charles Parquin was a firm believer in the point: "We always thrust with the point of our sabres, whereas [the English] always cut with their blade, which was three inches wide. Consequently, out of every twenty blows aimed by them, nineteen missed. But if the edge of the blade found its mark only once it was a terrible blow, and it was not unusual to see an arm cut clean from the body."

THE REVOLUTIONARY CALENDAR

In November 1793, with effect back-dated to September 1792, the French Republic abandoned the Gregorian calendar in favour of a newly devised Revolutionary system under which "Year One" (An I) began on 22 September 1792. Military equipment produced between that date and 22 December 1805, when Napoleon reverted to the Gregorian calendar, was designated accordingly:

Year II   (Sept.1793 -Sept.1794)
Year III   (Sept.1794 -Sept.1795)
Year IV   (Sept.1795 -Sept.1796)
Year V   (Sept.1796 -Sept.1797)
Year VI   (Sept.1797 -Sept.1798)
Year VII   (Sept.1798 -Sept.1799)
Year VIII (Sept.1799 -Sept.1800)
Year IX   (Sept.1800 - Sept.1801)
Year X   (Sept.1801 - Sept.1802)
Year XI   (Sept.1802 - Sept.1803)
Year XII   (Sept.1803 - Sept.1804)
Year XIII (Sept.1804 - Sept.1805)
Year XIV (Sept. - Dec.1805)

(**Left & below**) A Chasseur of c.1813 wearing the cavalry cloak – *manteau-capote* - introduced from that year. The previous models had been a voluminous hooded cloak, followed by the shorter three-quarter length *manteau trois-quarts* which lost the hood but gained a shoulder cape attached at the base of the collar, so that equipment belts could be worn over the cloak but under the cape. The 1813 model retained this useful feature, but added optional cuffed sleeves, and buttons up the front. Its generous cut allowed it to cover not only the rider but also a good deal of the horse's back, and the *portmanteau* attached behind his saddle - in which the trooper of the turn of the century had been supposed to carry a pair of trousers, gaiters, stockings, two shirts, forage cap, stable jacket, needles and thread, scissors, razor, awl, brush, wax, pipeclay, shoe buckles, bag of hair powder, curry comb, sponge, soap, two handkerchiefs and a nightcap. We may assume that a

good many of these items would have disappeared from the kit of a typical trooper of the later Empire.

(Right) A photograph posed after a print by Karl-Alex Wilke: our 1st Chasseur dressed for a long winter's march, with the shako - which tended to chafe uncomfortably - replaced by the forage cap or *bonnet de police*. Note also the cloth-covered buttons down the front of the manteau-capote.

(Below & below right) The bonnet de police was made in the dark green of the Chasseurs, and bore the branch badge of a buglehorn in white; braiding was supposed to be white, like the tassel, and piping in regimental facing colours, but variations have been illustrated. Although officially superceded by the *pokalem* cap (see next page) after 1812, the earlier style was still seen worn by veterans after that date. It was a punishable offence to be caught in camp without the head covered.

(**Right & below**) Stable dress laid down by the 1812 regulations consisted of a plain green stable jacket fastened with ten pewter buttons, without the regimentally faced collar and cuffs previously prescribed; and this *"pokalem"* forage cap, with ear/neck flaps which could be buttoned up or down, made in Chasseur dark green with regimental piping and a white regimental number. These were typically worn in barracks with rough, unbleached canvas stable trousers and wooden clogs; but on campaign many items were lost, worn out, or discarded, and our trooper wears his riding overalls. De Brack suggested that all a cavalryman should carry with him apart from his weapons and ammunition were his cloak, two spare shirts, sewing kit, an extra pair of boots, and whatever rations he required.

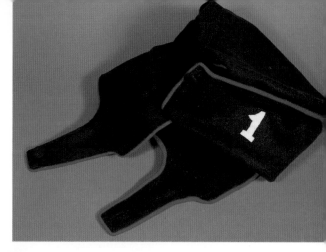

(Right) Chasseur trooper of the mid-to late Empire, his shako protected for winter campaigning by a black oilcloth cover with a tied-up neck flap, drinking from a natural gourd converted into a canteen. There was no official issue of canteens in the French army, and soldiers acquired many different types of flask and water bottle. There are some splendid examples of soldiers' engraved gourds in the Musée de l'Armée, Paris, and the Musée de l'Emperi, Salon de Provence.

(Left) A fine reproduction of the 1806 model shako with full dress plume and cords, produced by Louis Chalmers of "The Plumery", Chiswick, London. The chinscales were tied up behind the plume or pompon, or to a small hook at the back of the shako, when not in use. The lengths and exact colour combinations of plumes vary widely in period sources, usually showing green and regimental facing colour.

11

(Right) Napoleon's decree of 1 October 1801 established a *compagnie d'élite* within each of the Chasseur, Hussar and Dragoon regiments, following the pattern already established in the infantry. The élite company was to be the senior of the two companies which comprised the 1st Squadron. To mark their status the new élite companies were granted the right to wear bearskin *colpacks* (busbies), and flaming grenade insignia on turnbacks, buckle plates and cartridge pouches; other distinctions were red plumes, cords and tassels, and red epaulettes. Here men of the 1st Chasseurs Élite Company display both the retained dolman (left) and the conventional Kinski, with the new distinctions.

(Right) Demonstration by men of the recreated 1st Chasseurs Élite Company and British 1st Foot Guards Light Company of the relative reach of the Napoleonic light cavalryman and infantryman in hand-to-hand combat. The infantry, when isolated, were the favourite prey of the troopers: the bulk, height and speed of the horse gave them the physical and psychological advantage, and an individual on foot could usually be cut down - if the infantry were scattered and running - with murderous ease. But as long as the infantry held their regulation tight formations, and ideally the "square", cavalry were largely helpless against them, due to the much greater firepower of the massed muskets and the deterrent effect on the horses of the hedge of long bayonets.

(**Above & above right**) Rear view of the élite company colpack with its red "flame" or bag tasselled and piped in white. All light cavalry wore similar equipment in whitened buff leather (except for the 5th and 27th Chasseurs, which used natural leather). The two belts passed over the left shoulder, the broader carbine/musketoon sling overlaying the narrower sling supporting the cartridge pouch, the two being attached by a brass alloy stud; metal fittings were all brass alloy except for the steel spring clip which engaged with the carbine (see pages 43 & 45). Note again the three-bar hilt of the Year XI light cavalry sabre, its leather fist strap tightened round the wrist to prevent loss in action. Napoleon attempted to rationalise the many types of sidearm previously carried by the French cavalry.

(**Left**) An élite company trooper clears a jump in woodland.

(Left) The scarlet uniform decorations of the Élite Company, 1st Chasseurs - matched by the "wolf-tooth" or "vandyked" cloth edging his sheepskin saddle cover - are very striking in this sunlit study of a villainously moustachioed trooper.

(Below) A light cavalry mêlée: a trooper of the French 1st Chasseurs Élite Company parries a sabre cut from a trooper of the British 12th Light Dragoons in post-1812 uniform.

Although the overall record of the British cavalry during the Napoleonic Wars was less professionally impressive than that of their adversaries, they showed a proper light cavalry conceit; it is true that they were usually better mounted than the French, and there was a widespread belief that they cared for their horses better. The Frenchman Charles Parquin recounted an amusing story of one Monsieur Fage of the 13th Chasseurs who was pursuing an English officer, but could not close with him because of the splendid quality of the Englishman's horse. Remaining ten yards ahead of his pursuer, the Englishman turned to observe in a mocking tone, "I presume that is a Norman horse you are riding, Sir?" Enraged by his sarcasm, Fage drew and fired his pistol, only to suffer a misfire. "I presume", commented the Englishman,"that you get your weapons from the armament works at Versailles?"....

(Left & below) A subaltern officer of the 1st Chasseurs on campaign. He wears the 1810 model shako, his commissioned rank indicated by the silver lace band, and the plume replaced for campaign by a pompon in company colour - sky blue identified the 2nd Company of the 1st Squadron. His no doubt expensive, silver-laced pouch belt is protected on campaign by a red Morocco leather cover. He wears the comfortable and popular 1808 Kinski with the silver epaulette and counter-epaulette of his grade, over the fancy regimental *gilet* waistcoat. Note that these are trousers - which became popular during the Empire - not buttoned riding overalls. The trousers originally appeared in grey, but later in Chasseur green with two regimentally coloured stripes down the outer seams. Note the two-tone effect on his gauntlet gloves.

Veterans of Austerlitz, Auerstaedt and Wagram, the 1st Chasseurs served with the 1st Corps of the Grande Armée in 1812, and fought at Smolensk and Borodino. During the retreat from Moscow the horses of French officers and men alike suffered from the lack of the special snow horseshoes and - equally important - "caulkins" or snow nails; only the Imperial household had adequate supplies. It was generally believed by French farriers that snow shoes, being heavy, would tire the horses unecessarily; and that snow nails, which had raised heads for better grip, carried an unacceptable risk of injury if a rear hoof "overreached" and clipped a front leg, or if one horse kicked another, as is their nature.

As well as being treacherous going, the Russian snow naturally prevented the horses from grazing, and they starved in their tens of thousands. But it was not merely the weather which killed them: even during the advance of summer 1812 losses from exhaustion and ill-use were staggering - just 24 days into the campaign Murat could only mount some 14,000 of his 22,000 troopers. Ironically, it was only the horsemeat hacked from the cadavers which marked every few yards of the retreat that enabled the famished survivors of the Grande Armée - generally accepted as numbering some 15,000 men, out of about 450,000 - to stagger back to Poland.

15

(Left, above & opposite top)
A subaltern officer of the 7th Chasseurs displays the rose-coloured facings of the senior regiment of the third group on the collar, cuffs, piping and turnbacks of his Kinski; at the tip of his shako plume; and as seam stripes on his trousers. His 1806 pattern shako has the silver lace top band of officer rank, and is adorned with silver cords and tassels; the lozenge-shaped plate attached below the national cockade carries the buglehorn of the Chasseurs (also seen embroidered in silver on the jacket turnbacks) and the unit number.

The pouch belt and pouch are elaborately laced and decorated; this was the type of item by which officers tended to display their wealth in periods predating the modern attitude to regulation patterns and strict conformity. Pouch belts might be decorated with lion masks, chains, Imperial eagles, crowned Ns, or shields bearing regimental numbers.

The 7th, formerly the Chasseurs de Picardie, served at Jena and Eylau in 1806-7; at Wagram in 1809; in Spain in 1810-11, fighting at Fuentes d'Onoro; and with the Grande Armée in 1812-13, their many actions including Polotsk, the Berezina, Bautzen, and Leipzig.

Of the qualities demanded of a light cavalry officer, Gen. de Brack wrote: "A man must be born a light cavalry soldier. No situation requires...such an innate genius for war...The qualities which render a man superior - intelligence, willpower - ought to be found united in him. Left constantly to himself, exposed to constant fighting, responsible not only for the troops under his command but also to those which he is protecting and scouting for, every minute finds employment for his mental and bodily faculties. His profession is a rough one, but every day affords him opportunities for distinguishing himself, a glorious compensation which repays his toils so much the more, as it shows so much the sooner what he is worth..."

16

(**Below left & below**) Given the 1806 pattern shako, this *brigadier* (corporal) of the 1st Chasseurs in smart full dress uniform may perhaps be enjoying home service after the Austerlitz campaign; led by Col. Montbrun, the 1st served at Ulm, Amstetten, Mariazell and Austerlitz itself, where they captured six enemy cannon and were mentioned in two official bulletins for their bravery. Our NCO wears the dolman known to have been retained in the 1st Chasseurs, with the tight Hungarian-style laced breeches and laced and tasselled boots.

Handsome studies, taken outside Boulogne, of our corporal of the 1st Chasseurs mounted. The two white lace chevrons above the cuff mark his rank; the *maréchal-des-logis* and *maréchal-des-logis-chef* (sergeant and sergeant-major) wore one and two silver chevrons respectively.

(Right & below) The 1st Chasseurs dressing their ranks; and at the charge. Describing a charge by his 23rd Chasseurs in 1813 against Austrian Hussars, Marbot reports that his Élite Company threw the enemy column into such disorder that they turned and ran, and that the pursuit, which lasted more than an hour, cost the enemy 200 casualties without French loss. This is quite plausible, as fleeing troops were always notoriously vulnerable.

The horses themselves could be dangerous. Marbot's mount Lisette, enraged by a bayonet in the leg at Eylau, literally bit off a Russian soldier's face, trampled and kicked others, and disembowelled an officer who grabbed at her bridle. (The author, who has been picked up by the shoulder and flung across a stable simply because a horse was in a bad mood, finds the story entirely believable. While the horses used for re-enactment are usually well trained and docile, a sudden noise or even a piece of wind-blown paper can cause them to explode into panic with frightening speed and strength.)

Hussars

There were 13 regiments of Hussars in existence when Napoleon took up the reins of power in 1799. Three (7eme bis, 11eme and 12eme Hussards) would later be converted to Dragoons; the 11eme was reformed in 1810, the 12eme, 13eme and a new 14eme in 1813-14. The original six regiments had been mainly recruited from Alsace and Lorraine in the 18th century; their orders were issued in German until 1793, and in a bastard Alsatian dialect for years thereafter.

Hussars, as a class of troops, trace their origins to the far eastern frontiers where the Austro-Hungarian Empire faced the Ottoman Turks. The elements of their traditionally flamboyant costume - fur cap, lavishly braided and fur-trimmed jacket carried slung from the shoulder, the coloured "barrel sash" - became formalised into a recognisable uniform as they travelled west via Hungary and Germany to Western Europe.

In their tactical functions the Hussars were identical to their light cavalry comrades, the Chasseurs; but Hussars considered themselves distinctly more dashing than mere Chasseurs. They attracted audacious officers, like the young General Lasalle, who remarked that any Hussar who wasn't dead by the age of thirty was a blackguard; and it is hardly surprising that their reckless demeanour and sartorial splendour proved popular with the ladies. Conan Doyle's fictional but entirely convincing Hussar

Hussars of the recreated 7eme (left) and 5eme Hussards ride onto the field at the Waterloo commemoration in June 1995.

officer, Gerard, remarked that the appearance of Hussars could start a whole population running - the men away from them, and the women towards them...

One good reason to flee their arrival was the reputation of the unevenly-supplied French for looting, and light cavalry were often sent out to forage for the army. *Sous-lieutenant* Albert de Roca of the 2nd Hussars, who fought in Spain, recalled: "Hussars and Chasseurs were generally accused of being plunderers and prodigals, loving drink and fancying everything fair while in the presence of the enemy. Accustomed, one may almost say, to sleep with an eye open, to have an ear always alert to the sound of the trumpet, to reconnoitre far in advance during a march, to discover the enemy's ambuscades, to observe the slightest traces of their marches, to examine defiles, and to scan the plains with an eagle eye, they could not fail to have acquired superior intelligence and habits of independence. Nevertheless, they were always silent and submissive in the presence of their officers, for fear of being dismounted."

21

(**Left**) Eagle bearer of the 5th Hussars; in the light cavalry the eagles were usually carried by selected NCOs.

The regiment which would become the 5th Hussars was formed in 1783 from the cavalry of the volunteer "Lauzun's Legion", newly returned from service in the American War of Independence. Briefly numbered 6, the regiment took its final number in 1793.

The Hussar regiments were distinguished one from another by a bewilderingly complex - some would say, anarchic - variety of coloured uniform items and facings. The 5th wore the dolman jacket and breeches or overalls in sky blue; the cuffs and the *pelisse* overjacket were white; and the braid and lace was yellow or gold, depending upon rank. In the matter of headgear, the regulations changed several times during the Empire, and period sources show that Hussar regiments were in any case a law unto themselves. This is the 1806 model shako in its early style, furnished with cords, a pompon and a cockade but no plate, and covered in regimentally coloured cloth.

(**Below**) Detail of the enlisted men's sabretache of the 5th Hussars. Originally these flat leather pouches with deep, ornately decorated flaps, carried hanging from the sabre belt, served to carry writing and sketching materials in the field; by this date they were largely decorative, particularly for the often illiterate common soldiers.

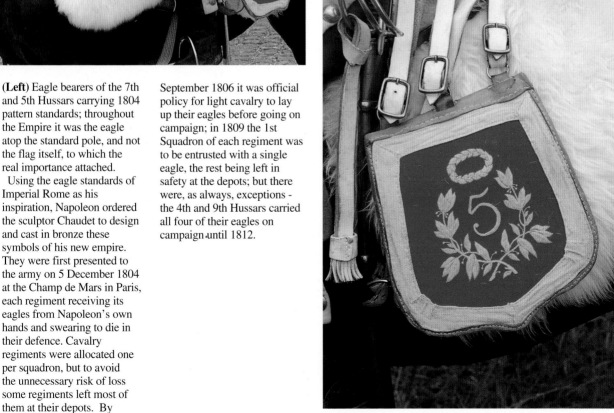

(**Left**) Eagle bearers of the 7th and 5th Hussars carrying 1804 pattern standards; throughout the Empire it was the eagle atop the standard pole, and not the flag itself, to which the real importance attached.

Using the eagle standards of Imperial Rome as his inspiration, Napoleon ordered the sculptor Chaudet to design and cast in bronze these symbols of his new empire. They were first presented to the army on 5 December 1804 at the Champ de Mars in Paris, each regiment receiving its eagles from Napoleon's own hands and swearing to die in their defence. Cavalry regiments were allocated one per squadron, but to avoid the unnecessary risk of loss some regiments left most of them at their depots. By September 1806 it was official policy for light cavalry to lay up their eagles before going on campaign; in 1809 the 1st Squadron of each regiment was to be entrusted with a single eagle, the rest being left in safety at the depots; but there were, as always, exceptions - the 4th and 9th Hussars carried all four of their eagles on campaign until 1812.

(Right & opposite) Eagle
bearer of the recreated 7th
Hussars; he wears the later
style 1806 pattern shako as
worn c.1807-1812, with the
lozenge-shaped plate
bearing an eagle motif over
a cut-out regimental number.
The 7th wore a dark green
dolman with scarlet collar
and cuffs, a dark green
pelisse, and yellow or
gold braid and lace. This man
wears riding overalls in
regimental green with red
striping.

With Napoleon's return to
power in 1815 came the need
for new eagle standards for
his reassembled squadrons.
These were similar in style
to the earlier eagles but of
simpler design; one was
presented to each regiment.
However, some of the earlier
Imperial eagles were still in
existence; and the 3rd
Hussars, 5th Lancers and 7th
Cuirassiers all carried their
former eagles into the
Hundred Days campaign.
The 7th Hussars fought at
Fleurus and Waterloo under
the command of Colonel
Marbot, who had preserved
the eagle of his former
regiment, the 23rd
Chasseurs à Cheval. This
eagle can still be seen in the
Musée de l'Armée, with the
number 7 attached to the
plinth, but with the holes from
the old numerals 23 still
visible.

(Right) Detail of the
sabretache design of the 7th
Hussars, in this case that of a
member of the separate group
which recreates the
Compagnie d'Élite.

Maréchal-des-logis of the 5th Hussars in the grounds of the imposing chateau of Montmirail. He wears campaign dress, and the dismounted study allows a good view of the riding overalls *(pantalons à cheval, or charivari)* typically worn by horsemen of all Napoleonic armies. They are reinforced up the inside of the legs and around the cuffs with leather, to protect the legs from chafing and the fabric from wear during long weeks spent almost constantly in the saddle. French overalls had 18 pewter or bone buttons up the outside, set in stripes of regimental colour; the overalls could be unbuttoned up the outside and removed without taking the boots off - they were supposed to be worn over, not instead of, the breeches. The fancy-shaped downwards buttoning pocket flaps with piped edges are also typical.

The dolman was worn on campaign in temperate weather; the pelisse was substituted in colder weather. Note the gold lace rank chevron with narrow red backing above the dolman cuffs; and the single plain gold service chevron on the left upper sleeve only, indicating at least eight years in the army (see also page 28).

(Left) 5th Hussar trooper in dolman and bonnet de police. These caps appear in the contemporary sources in all combinations of regimental uniform, facing and lace colours. He is carrying his saddle, with its portmanteau and sheepskin cover attached.

(Below left) Dreaming of home, and the sweetheart he left behind, this man wears the pale blue stable jacket of the 5th Hussars.

(Opposite top) An officer of the 5th Hussars smokes a peaceful pipe by the chateau woodpile. He wears the regiment's sky blue dolman partly open over a gold-laced red gilet, and has thrown his white pelisse over his shoulders against the evening chill; note the details of his gold-laced forage cap.

This superb example of light cavalry splendour may tempt us to forget that theirs was as serious a business as that of any Napoleonic soldier. De Roca of the 2nd Hussars - deployed to Spain in 1808, and renowned for their successful charge, alongside the Vistula Lancers, against Colborne's British infantry brigade at Albuera - left this memory:

"The habit of danger made us look upon death as one of the most ordinary circumstances of life. We pitied our comrades when wounded, but once they had ceased to live the indifference which was shown them amounted almost to irony. When, as the soldiers passed by, they recognised one of their companions stretched among the dead, they said 'He wants for nothing now - he will not be able to abuse his horse any more - he has got drunk for the last time', or something similar, which only marked in the speaker a stoical contempt of existence. Such were the only funeral orations pronounced in honour of those who fell..."

(Below) Another angle on the 5th Hussars' dolman and bonnet de police, showing braid and lace details. Note again the rank and service chevrons worn by this NCO; for ranks below sergeant the former were in yellow in this unit, and the latter in red throughout the army.

(Below) Dawn patrol: with the first rays of the rising sun, a cavalry patrol moves towards a farmhouse on the horizon. This photograph was taken during the "Campaign de France", an extremely enjoyable and challenging event organised by Jean-Pierre Mir of the Hussards de Lasalle, and based on the Chateau de Montmirail. After an initial open day for the public the recreated infantry, cavalry and artillery all go out on campaign, travelling 25km away from Montmirail, then fighting a battle each day over some of the battlefields of 1814 - Champaubert, Montmirail and Vauchamps among them. The nights are spent in period barns and haylofts or under the stars, wrapped in a manteau-capote with a shako for a pillow.

Officer of the 5th Hussars in campaign dress: dolman alone, his ornate white pelisse being left with the baggage cart; overalls; plain black sabretache with brass eagle and number; slung flask and spyglass case; and *shabraque* devoid of expensive ornaments and eagle patches, too easy to damage or dirty in the field.

(Right) A trooper of the 5th gives a good demonstration of the "military seat": his legs are almost straight due to the long length of his stirrup leathers, and if he rose to stand in the stirrups he would only clear the saddle by a couple of inches. In general, greys such as this were reserved for trumpeters, who needed to be highly visible to their officers at all times; but by the late Empire - especially after 1812 - cavalrymen took what horses they could get.

(Right) Sergeant of the 5th at speed, sabre in hand. In 1806 this regiment and the 7th, forming General Lasalle's brigade, covered 1160km (720 miles) in 25 days in pursuit of the defeated Prussians. They also bluffed the 6,000-man garrison of Stettin into surrendering, along with 160 guns.

(**Left & below**) An officer of the 7th Hussars in the manteau-capote. This was essentially similar for both officers and men, though naturally of better materials for the former, who purchased their own; this officer has his cape lined with the regiment's red facing colour.

(**Right & below**) Captain of the 7th Hussars wearing the officer's gold-braided shako, dolman, overalls and saddle furniture; note the handsome gold-laced red leather equipment and "mameluke"-style sabre. Under the 1812 regulations all Hussar regiments were to wear green breeches and manteaux, in the interests of economy; it can easily be imagined what regiments with other traditional colours thought of this idea, and many disregarded this and any subsequent orders which attempted to turn them into mere Chasseurs.

(Below) A moment's relaxation on the march for a veteran officer. The gold *galons* above the cuffs of his superb dolman indicate captain's rank.

(Right) Captain of 7th Hussars in barracks or a billet, relaxing over a pipe while attended by a regimental *cantiniére*. Note the richness of his gold-laced forage cap and waistcoat.

(Above & opposite)
Beautifully reconstructed equipment of a captain of the 7th Hussars. The boots are of authentic construction with a "concertina" effect sewn into the insteps for greater comfort; note gold lace and tassels, shaped cut of upper edges, and gilt rowelled block spurs. His green pelisse is of high quality woollen cloth, richly laced and braided with gold and trimmed with thick brown fur. The shako is covered with green cloth and gold lace; a button and gold cord with a large boss secure the national cockade. The face of the full dress sabretache bears gold and silver bullion embroidery and an applied gilt eagle; the pouch and belt are of gold-laced red Morocco.

Note the dark bearskin colpack, with red bag, and the red plume of the élite company. In fact many French officers of centre companies chose to wear the colpack in preference to the shako, considering it more martial in appearance but also better balanced and more comfortable than the shako. In 1812 new regulations required élite companies of Hussar regiments to give up the colpack and adopt the same red-braided shako as had replaced the bearskin in the infantry's grenadier companies. The light cavalry - needless to add - resisted the change.

(**Left & above**) The Élite Company of the 7th Hussars is recreated by a separate re-enactment group. Here a trooper poses in regimental full dress of green dolman and pelisse and scarlet Hungarian-style breeches with yellow lace decoration on the thighs, with the red-plumed, yellow-corded colpack of the compagnies d'elite. Note the linen lining and yellow toggled cord attachment of the trooper's pelisse.

(**Above & right**) Left side of
the colpack showing the
tasselled bag or "flame"; note
also the black fleece trim of
the trooper's quality pelisse,
its rear decoration, the stripes
on the breeches, and the
regimental sabretache.

(Left) Maréchal-des-logis of the 7th Hussars Élite Company in stable dress according to the 1812 regulations - a single-breasted jacket, without facings, closed by ten pewter buttons. Before this date the stable jacket - worn for all dirty chores to prevent soiling the expensive dolman - could be either single- or double-breasted with eight or nine buttons per row. Rough linen or canvas trousers were worn for such duties, and often wooden clogs in place of boots. This sergeant carries a light cavalry bridle.

(Below) The sheepskin cover over the Hungarian-style saddle, held in place by the leather surcingle and counterstrap; the cantle protrudes through the sheepskin. The cover was a necessary aid for the rider's comfort, given the great distances covered by light cavalry on campaign and the time spent in the saddle. It did have drawbacks, however: in warm weather it was uncomfortably hot to ride on; and in rain it soaked up water like a sponge, leading to rotting of the sheepskin and of anything which was in contact with it, such as leather straps and the rider's overalls.

(Right) The very portrait of a hussar: the 7th Hussars Élite Company sergeant-major, identified as the maréchal-des-logis-chef by the two gold chevrons above his dolman cuffs. He wears the dolman open over his red gilet and barrel-sash.

Soldier of the 7th Hussars Élite Company in cold weather campaign dress, wearing his pelisse instead of his dolman. He displays a red pompon rather than the full dress plume in his colpack; and his red breeches are protected by leather-reinforced overalls buttoning up the outside leg. Note (left) the campaign cover over his sabretache, in plain black oilcloth with a painted number; and (right) the carbine carried attached to its sling by a spring clip and butt-strap. This trooper carries the earlier pattern of Hussar sabre.

(**Above & left**) The regulations stated that all ranks should be issued with a pair of pistols, which were carried butt-forward in saddle holsters covered by the sheepskin. In practice, due to general shortages of pistols, only officers, trumpeters, and (if they were lucky) NCOs usually managed to get a brace. Troopers counted themselves lucky to be issued with a single pistol, of the Year IX model; the Year XIII was rare, and old 1763 or 1777 patterns or captured foreign models were more common. The single pistol was usually carried in the left holster, and horse brushes and hoof picks in the right. Here a sergeant loads a 1777 pistol; this had an exposed 189mm barrel of 17.1mm bore, and originally came fitted with a belt hook. As with all muzzle-loading flintlock weapons, fixed

ammunition was carried in the form of a folded paper tube containing a ball and powder charge. This cartridge was bitten open; some priming powder was poured into the external pan, which was closed by the spring-loaded frizzen; the rest of the powder was poured down the muzzle, and the ball tamped home on it with the ramrod, the cartridge paper acting as wadding. Reloading in the saddle was seldom practical during an engagement.

When pistols were used in combat the sabre was allowed to hang from the wrist by its fist strap or "sword knot"; some veterans preferred to substitute a large knotted kerchief for the strap, as this could also be wrapped round the hand to give a degree of protection. After firing, the pistol would be quickly transferred to the left hand and the sabre recovered.

(Above & right) The carbine ("musketoon") - here the Year IX pattern - was carried by engaging the spring clip on the sling with a ring sliding free along a bracket attached to the left side of the weapon; a butt-strap further secured it. The carbine could be fired from the shoulder without disengaging the clip from the sliding ring. Firing a volley from the saddle was a recognised method of disrupting approaching enemy cavalry, but the results were not always predictable. Parquin recalled an action at Eylau when heavy casualties were caused by a volley held until enemy dragoons were only a few yards away; but at Sahagun the British 15th Hussars overthrew two French regiments who, believing them to be Spanish cavalry who "never charge home", tried unsuccessfully to check them by firepower only to be caught at the halt and broken.

(Right) A splendid woodland study of a sergeant-major, wearing the forage cap in the alternative manner to that shown on page 28 - with the "flame" hanging free, rather than folded up inside the "turban" with only the tassel exposed.

(Above) 7th Hussars at the trot. As well as the prestige, men of the Élite Company also received an extra sou a day - known as the "sou of the grenade", after the traditional badge of elite companies in the French army.

(Right) A trooper at the charge. Gen.de Brack claimed that "the cavalryman charging is...actuated by one all-pervading feeling which is almost intoxicating"; but he went on to say that care must be taken not to weaken the effect of this mood, which was both subtle and fleeting.

(Above) 8th Hussars officer in undress, and dismounted sentry in full dress. This regiment wore basically the same uniform as the 7th but with white and silver lace in place of yellow and gold; the troopers' dolmans and pelisses were sometimes (though not here) further differenced by the substitution of red and black lace, and the trumpeters wore a striking all-red uniform instead of the usual reversed colours, with a green and black barrel sash and black fur trim on the pelisse. Note here the two usual styles of lace thigh decoration on the breeches: the officer has the simple "pic" shape, the trooper the more complex "Hungarian knot".

(**Above & left**) 8th Hussars officer on the field of battle, wearing a very dark green uniform. He rides with a simplified green shabraque, and his sabretache has a red leather cover with applied eagle and number. The 8th, formed in 1793, were at Austerlitz in 1805, at Jena in 1806 and Eylau in 1807, at Aspern-Essling and Wagram in 1809, at Borodino in 1812 and Leipzig in 1813. After the actions at Danzig, Strasbourg and Champaubert in 1814 they were disbanded in May that year, and were not reformed for the 1815 campaign.

Veterinaries and Farriers

In theory, five years was the minimum age for a cavalry mount in the French army, although in practice younger horses were taken into service as the natural wastage of repeated campaigns made the problem of providing remounts increasingly serious. The nadir was reached in 1813 after the appalling losses of the Russian campaign, when the army had just 15,000 largely untrained horses of which only about 3,000 were judged suitable and ready for cavalry service. Napoleon's attitude to horseflesh was as coldly practical as it was towards his men: "...[Cavalry] should not be handled with any miserly instinct to keep it intact... I do not wish the horses to be spared if they catch men...Take no heed of the complaints of the cavalry, for if such great objects may be obtained as the destruction of a whole enemy army, the state can afford to lose a few hundred horses from exhaustion...."

The day-to-day duty of maintaining the cavalry's mounts in the field fell to the regimental farriers; only at a farrier's request would a horse be examined by the regiment's single veterinary. Although these latter were graduates of the Écoles Hippiatriques at Alfort or Lyon, they could not attain a higher rank than sergeant.

Period veterinary practice including the bleeding of sick animals; and the collecting together of any debilitated animals for care - which had the unfortunate effect of spreading contagion among animals many of which might only be suffering initially from lameness or some other relatively minor complaint.

It was the sergeant-farrier's job to inspect the condition of the horses at each of the three daily grooming parades, or at each of the prescribed halts on the march to rest the horses and re-adjust girths, surcingles and other tack. Whenever a horse is working the girth strap, which fastens the saddle to the horse, becomes slack; if it is not checked and retightened the time will come when a sudden movement, with the consequent redistribution of the rider's weight, will cause the saddle to slip round the horse's body and dump the careless trooper under its hooves. The farriers, who shoed the horses, also rode at the tail of the pelotons to pick up any horseshoes which might be cast on the march.

(Left above) Front and rear detail of the silver lacing and furniture of the 8th Hussars officer's dolman, gilet, breeches, and pouch belt.

(Left below) A hook-and-eye enabled the shabraque to be fastened in this position when in the field, to protect its embroidered decoration. The inside of the shabraque was often lined with blue and white striped ticking material.

(Right above) As the first step in shoeing the farrier removes the worn-out shoe, taking care not to damage the outer "crust" of the hoof in the process.

(Right) Next the excess growth is cleaned from the hoof with the rasp, and a good surface is prepared to accept the new shoe.

Saddles and Bridles

Many reconstructed cavalry units ride with modern tack; others have developed saddles and bridles which resemble the originals, but with "softer" bits to avoid unnecessary damage to the horses' mouths. Modern stables would not be happy to hire out mounts to be ridden with period bits, which were extremely severe - as they had to be, when an out-of-control horse could mean the rider's certain death.

Napoleonic cavalry all rode to battle with double reins and bits. A bridoon (small ringed snaffle) was fitted snugly into the corners of the mouth; then a curb bit *(mors de bride)* was added, positioned to rest on the bars of the mouth just below the snaffle, at least half an inch above the tushes or two inches above the corner incisors when there were no tushes. The curb chain was twisted flat, then hooked at such a length that the branches of the bit formed an angle of 45 degrees with the lower jaw when the reins were lightly stretched; the rein passed below the snaffle. If the curb chain was too loose the bit "fell through" and lost its curb effect, acting like the snaffle on the corners of the mouth; if it was too tight the horse became fretful, repeatedly throwing its head as it sought to escape the constant pressure.

(**Left**) The farrier was a skilled specialist: a carelessly placed nail could render a horse unserviceable. Normal wear and hoof growth required the replacement of shoes approximately once a month. Shoes began life as long, straight metal bars, which were cut and hammered into shape using portable forges carried with the regimental supply wagons. To judge if the filed surface of the hoof was flat enough to accept the new shoe, the latter was first heated hot enough to leave scorch marks on any raised areas when offered up to the hoof. These were then rasped flat, and any necessary alterations made to the shoe on the farrier's anvil. A final check was made with the reheated shoe, which could then be nailed into place; nails were driven through the insensitive outer crust of the hoof and then bent over with the hammer to form the "clench".

(**Above right**) Reconstruction of an officer's bridle with the twin reins and bits. Officers' tack and horse furniture was often decorated with more or less elaborate embellishments, depending upon rank and personal wealth.

(**Right**) Close-up of the Napoleonic bitting arrangement; from this it can be seen that there is greater leverage against the horse's mouth from the lower (curb) rein, so this must be used lightly. The curb bit is decorated here with Medusa-head bosses.

(Top left) A trooper's "Hungarian" light cavalry saddle; holsters are attached at the front and horseshoe cases at the rear. The set of the wooden trees kept the weight clear of the horse's spine, and the seat nailed and laced in place between the pommel (front) and cantle (rear) could be covered by a quilted cushion. Without adequate padding with horse blankets, however, the wooden trees would soon rub a horse's back raw, causing suppurating wounds; given the weight of equipment and the fact that French cavalrymen seldom dismounted to lead, it is not surprising that in the Peninsula the British claimed that a French patrol up-wind could be smelt before it was seen. Worse than routine neglect through ignorance was the coward's trick of slipping pebbles under the saddle blanket to deliberately injure the horse, so that the rider could be sent safely to the rear to await a remount.

(Far left) The crupper strap, which passed under the horse's tail to prevent the saddle slipping forwards.

(Left) Cantle of the Hungarian saddle from the rear, showing the strapping arrangement for attachment of the crupper and the portmanteau.

(Above left & above) A cavalry officer's saddle, covered in leather and finished to a higher standard than those of the rankers. The side trees are padded and covered with leather to help prevent pressure sores on the backs of officers' expensive chargers.

(Right) Detail of another officer's saddle; note stirrup iron and method of adjusting stirrup leather, and brass studding - like most items of equipment before the Industrial Revolution, saddles showed many slight variations due to dispersed manufacture and personal purchase.

Weapons

(**Right**) The Napoleonic cavalryman's primary weapon - outside the relatively few lancer regiments - was his sabre. These were curved for the light cavalry, in the style directly traceable to the Middle Eastern sword of the medieval period; and straight for the heavy regiments, following the tradition which led from the medieval broadsword to the 18th century German cavalry *Pallasch*. These are three Year XI light cavalry sabres, the universal issue to the Hussars, Chasseurs and Lancers.

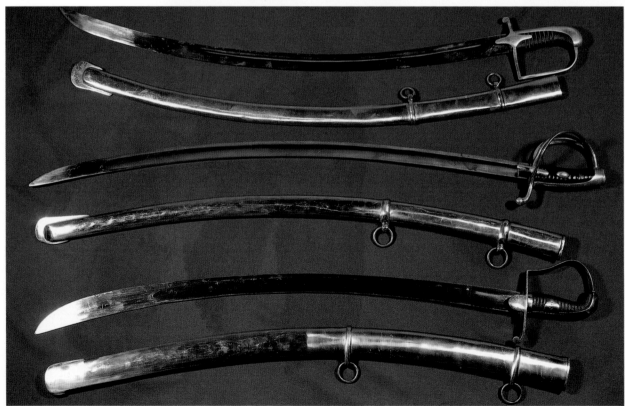

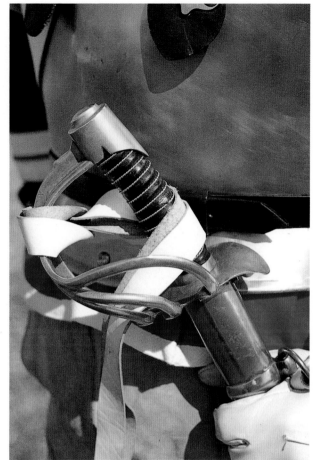

(Left) Comparison of an early French light cavalry sabre with a simple knucklebow hilt (top), with the Year XI sabre with three-bar hilt (centre), and a British 1796 light cavalry sabre. The latter has a wider blade and a hatchet point. In the Peninsular campaign a French officer actually lodged an official complaint against the horrific slashing wound inflicted by the British weapon. An excellent exhibit can still be seen in the Musée de l'Armée, Paris - a sabre-slashed shako which belonged to Col.Marbot of the 23rd Chasseurs and 7th Hussars.

(Above) A straight-bladed Year XII Dragoon sabre in its black leather scabbard with brass alloy fittings. The leather-covered grip is wrapped with wire. An earlier version of this sword had iron fittings.

(Above right) The Cuirassier's Year XI sabre is housed in an iron scabbard; it has a 97cm blade with a twin gutter, total sheathed length being 120cm. Officers carried either a straight or a gently curved *sabre de bataille*.

(Right) A reconstructed 1786 model carbine, 115cm in length; its accuracy, while obviously better than that of the pistols, still left much to be desired. This type was slowly replaced by the Year IX pattern during the Empire (compare with page 45 - the spacing of the fore end bands is the easiest identifying feature), but many earlier and foreign carbines were also issued. The carbine took a bayonet, which is referred to in some contemporary documents as on issue; but there is no pictorial evidence for their carriage or use by light cavalry - which would seem impractical for troops already armed with sabres - and they remain something of a mystery.

(Left) Reconstructed saddle holsters for pistols.

(Right) Displayed against a 7th Hussar officer's effects, pistols of 1777 pattern (top) and Year IX pattern - the latter most quickly distinguishable from the generally similar 1763 type by its slanting brass priming pan.

(Below) Firing the 1777 pistol, turned on its left side so that the priming pan is vertically above the touch hole and the main charge in the barrel - an aid to reliable ignition, but no guarantee of it. As with all flintlocks, the cock holding the flint snaps forward when the trigger is pulled, simultaneously knocking the spring-loaded frizzen forward to expose the priming, and striking sparks from it to fall into the priming powder, which in theory should flare and detonate the main charge via the touch hole. Marshal Saxe, the great 18th century general, claimed never to have seen a pistol kill anything but a disabled horse; and pistols were widely believed to be useless unless "you feel your antagonist's ribs with the muzzle".

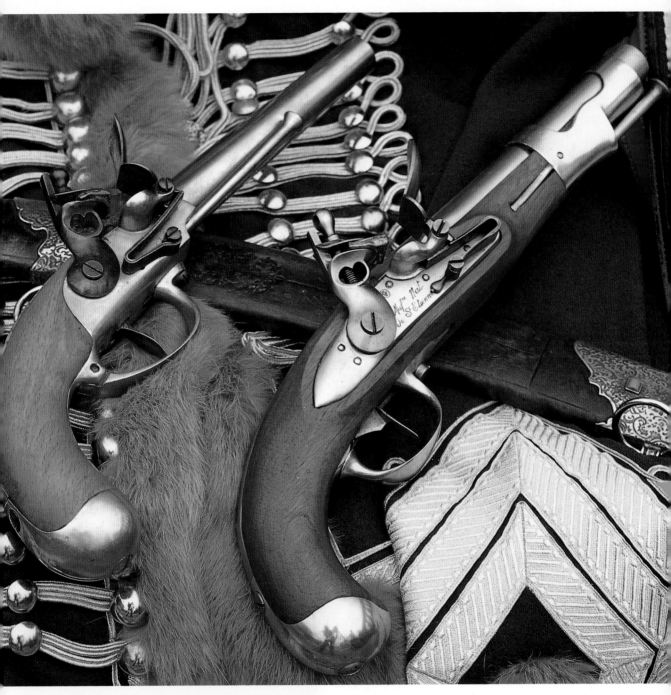

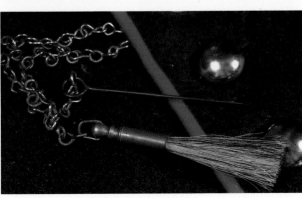

(Left) Pricker and brush - the latter often made of brass wire - to clean the touch hole and pan of flintlock weapons of the heavy fouling of burnt powder residue which quickly built up after a few shots.

The Vistula Lancers

A decree of March 1808 transferred the "Légion Polacco-Italienne" from the service of Westphalia to that of France; the corps, initially of one lancer and three infantry regiments, was renamed the Legion of the Vistula, with precedence equal to that of French Line Infantry and Chasseurs à Cheval. These Polish soldiers fought with notable spirit in the Peninsular campaigns, particularly in the siege of Saragossa and at Albuera. Colonel Jan Konopka took the 1st Vistula Lancers to Spain late in 1808; they served mostly under Suchet in the east of the country, and the marshal had their élite company provide him with a lancer escort. They were the first regiment of Polish lancers in French service; the Chevau-Légers Polonais de la Garde were raised in March 1807 but did not become Chevau-Légers Lanciers until 1809.

One of the most famous charges of the Napoleonic Wars was delivered by the Vistula Lancers - supported by the French 2nd Hussars - at Albuera on 16 May 1811. Charging under cover of a rainstorm and powder smoke, they caught Colborne's British infantry brigade in line formation; their muskets rendered useless by the rain, the three leading British battalions (1/3rd Buffs, 2/48th Northamptons and 2/66th Berkshires) were overrun and suffered between 85 and 60 per cent casualties. Of 80 officers and 1,568 men on the strength of the three battalions that morning, just 22 officers and 378 men remained unwounded in the ranks a few minutes after the Poles charged home. Although seriously wounded the colonel's younger brother, Captain Wincenty Konopka, captured one of several British colours lost in the action; in all Albuera cost the regiment 160 men out of 591. Lancers were the ideal troops to send against infantry in anything but unshaken square formation; and "in open country no fugitive on foot could escape a lancer".

(Above) In the hands of a well-trained man on a well-schooled horse the lance was a terrible weapon, both couched for a charge home and thrown like a spear (there are eyewitness descriptions of this tactic). Sergeant James Anton of the 42nd Highlanders, who fought French lancers at Quatre Bras on 16 June 1815, remembered: "Of all descriptions of cavalry, certainly the lancers seem the most formidable to infantry, as the lance can be projected with considerable precision and with deadly effect without bringing the horse to the point of a bayonet; and it was only by the rapid and well directed fire of musketry that these formidable assailants were repulsed." The great reach afforded by the 2.76m (9ft) lance also made the lancer deadly to other cavalry armed only with sabres. Note here the silhouette at his right stirrup iron of the strapped-on leather "bucket" which supported the butt end of the lance on the march.

(Right & opposite) On the march the lance could be carried "slung" as here, leaving both hands free for the management of the horse or the use of firearms. Here the pennon floats proudly; in the field they were often furled around the shaft and enclosed by a tubular waterproof cover. Note the piped rear details of the *kurtka* jacket; the carbine sling and pouch belt; the characteristic fabric "girdle" striped in unit colours; and the rolled cloak worn slung in such a way as to give some protection against sword cuts to the left rear torso, especially the kydney area, where troopers were taught to strike when pursuing enemy riders. When soldiers were given the order to "roll cloaks" they knew that battle was imminent.

(**Right & below**) In 1809 a 2nd Regiment of Lancers joined the Vistula Legion in the Peninsula. Their uniform was similar to that of the 1st, but had a blue collar and cuffs piped with yellow rather than the solid yellow of the premier regiment. Both units wore the traditional Polish lancer's headgear: the square-topped *czapka* helmet, of leather with a fabric crown reinforced with cane, the peak bound with brass. The Polish cross was worn superimposed on the French national cockade offset to the left front.

(Left) Lancers' kurtka jackets had plastron chests which could be buttoned across for extra warmth and to hide the facings, leaving only this piped edge showing. The general style of the kurtka was copied by the British army when new uniforms were prescribed for the Light Dragoon regiments in 1812.

When Napoleon decided to form Line Lancer regiments within the French army (see page 72) the 1st and 2nd Vistula Lancers became the 7th and 8th Light Horse Lancers. In 1815 Napoleon attempted to re-raise his Polish lancers for the Hundred Days campaign; the 7eme Chevau-Légers Lanciers Polonais were raised at Soissons, with 23 officers, 327 men, but unfortunately only 13 horses. The unit fought as infantry, defending the Sevres bridge on the outskirts of Paris in July 1815.

(Right) The only problem faced by lancers was what to do if an enemy got past the lance point and closed in with a sabre; if the lancer could not immediately extend the combat distance again, he was left trying frantically to parry the sword with his lance shaft. In a swirling mêlée he might throw his lance and draw his own sabre, but this took time - as anyone can attest who has tried to grope with the right hand across the width of the torso and down the left side to the hilt of a sabre dangling and flapping at the end of its slings. One option was to arm the second rank with sabres only, enabling them to exploit the gaps in the enemy formation punched by the initial impact of the lance-armed first rank. In an attempt to capitalise on the lancers' potential Marshal Marmont proposed that lances should be issued to the front ranks of all cavalry regiments, including the Cuirassiers; Napoleon decided against this, however.

Dragoons

Historically the Dragoons were mounted infantry, riding to the battlefield but dismounting to fight on foot. By the time of the Napoleonic Wars there was a general trend throughout Europe to employ Dragoons as conventional cavalry rather than dismounting them. However, the periodic French shortage of cavalry horses led to the formation of dismounted units of Dragons à Pied on several occasions. Five brigades, each comprising two squadrons from each of three regiments, were formed at the Boulogne invasion camp in 1803; a division of four regiments was formed on the Rhine in 1805; Massena briefly raised a single battalion in Italy the same year; and two regiments were raised and attached to the Imperial Guard in Germany in autumn 1806. All these formations were intended to be temporary, and once enough enemy horses had been captured to remount them those of 1805-6 were disbanded. When serving on foot the Dragoons wore long gaiters and shoes instead of their riding boots.

The Dragoons were the largest mounted arm, having 30 numbered regiments at their peak (1803-11). They were relatively inexpensive, generally receiving the least impressive of the available horses; and, being issued with a musket more effective than the cavalryman's carbine, they were usefully versatile - particularly in the endless struggle against the *guerrilleros* of the Peninsula, where no less than 25 regiments (all but the 7th, 23rd, 28th, 29th and 30th) served at one time or another.

They also fought as regular line-of-battle cavalry on many fields, however; and it was the Dragoon regiments in Spain which provided Napoleon with his last reserve of trained cavalrymen in 1813, when he ordered each unit to provide one or two squadrons to put some steel back into his cavalry in central Europe, ruined by the Russian disaster. They made their presence felt on the field of Dresden, among other actions, where they broke the Austrian infantry and overthrew their cavalry.

(**Left**) Wearing the 1804 regulation uniform, of which the most distinctive features were the crested and turbanned brass alloy helmet and the green *habit* coat, a farrier of the 2nd Dragoons (note his sleeve badges) stands guard above the English Channel. Regiments were distinguished by coloured facings; the large number of units meant that five groups of six regiments each shared the same colours: respectively scarlet for the 1st to 6th Dragoons, crimson for the 7th to 12th, then pink, yellow and orange. Within each group units had different applications of the colour on collars, lapels, cuffs, cuff flaps and tail turnbacks, some areas being coloured, others of green piped with the facing colour; the horizontal or vertical placing of the false pockets on the skirts also varied.

(Below) The whole branch wore helmets of brass alloy in a pseudo-Classical shape; a hollow crest with an embossed front plate supported a horsehair mane with a frontal tuft, and the skull was surrounded by a fur turban - usually brown cowhide, though officers sometimes displayed more expensive materials. The chinstrap was protected by brass alloy scales, and the leather peak was sometimes bound with brass. Details of helmet construction and decoration varied widely. For formal dress a plume - again, of many and often apparently arbitrary colour combinations - was added to the holder on the left side.

(Above) There were 33 pewter buttons on the habit, in two sizes: seven small buttons on each lapel, three on each cuff flap and one on each shoulder strap, and three of larger size on each pocket, two in the small of the rear waist, and three at the top of the right hand skirt. The buttons bore the regimental number. The 1804 habit was cut away sharply on the chest, and worn over a white waistcoat. During its lifetime the cut of the habit gradually became closer and shorter, and the turnbacks became false; a commonly seen alternative was a plain single-breasted *surtout.* From 1812 the habit was replaced officially by the *habit-veste,* which lost the cutaway front and fastened down to the waist; it had much shorter skirts, but retained the scheme of identifying facings. Note here details of the farrier's sleeve badge, and the shoulder strap of "duck's foot" shape.

(Above, left & opposite)
Left side and rear details of the
uniform and equipment. The
whitened cross belt over the
left shoulder supports the
musket cartridge pouch (see
left); below this was rolled and
strapped - rather insecurely in
this case - the green forage cap
decorated with white lace and
facing-coloured piping,
bearing in white or facing
colour the frontal badge of a
flaming grenade. The other
belt is the sword belt, which
was worn either around the
waist or - when on dismounted
duty - as a second cross belt. It
supported the scabbards for
both the straight Dragoon sabre
and the bayonet for the musket.

(Inset opposite) Detail of the
buttoning strap securing the
boots to the breeches; note
below this the stout cloth
manchette or boot-hose, worn
as a protection against chafing.

(**Left & right**) Our 2nd Dragoon in the saddle at the Waterloo commemoration event, 1995. Note the flaming grenade turnback badge of the whole Dragoon branch; and the regulation shabraque and holster covers - on campaign a sheepskin cover would have been added, and the rider would have worn buttoned and leather-reinforced overalls of grey or some other drab cloth.

Since we have mentioned the French cavalry's reputation for indifferent care of their horses, it is only fair to include here the story told by Sergeant Burgogne of Dragoon Mellé, who during the retreat from Moscow regularly slipped into the Russian horse lines to steal fodder for his mount Cadet; on another occasion he was seen on top of a burning barn, pulling straw from the roof for his horse. Mellé often marched dismounted, leading Cadet; and made holes in the ice with a hatchet to get him a drink. This admirable soldier remarked "If I save my horse, he will save me", and his record proved it: Cadet carried him safely through the campaigns in Italy, Prussia and Poland in 1805-07, in Germany in 1809, in Spain in 1808 and 1810-11, to Moscow and back in 1812-13 and in the campaign of France in 1813-14. Mellé was finally wounded, and Cadet killed under him, on the field of Waterloo.

(**Left & right**) Under the Consulate the French Dragoons were issued with infantry muskets. These were later progressively replaced by the Year IX or Year XI patterns of Dragoon musket, which differed little from one another, and from the infantry pattern only in being shortened by some 70mm from the muzzle for the sake of notionally easier handling on horseback. A small leather "bucket" was issued as part of the tack, hanging on straps from the right side of the saddle pommel below the pistol holster; the official way to carry the musket was to insert the end of the buttstock in this bucket, the barrel slanting up and back to be secured loosely by a strap from the cantle. In practice the musket seems to have been as often carried slung across the rider's back when in the field.

Note the characteristic way of wearing the chinscales tied up over the helmet peak.

Gendarmes

The Gendarmes acted as a military police force and were used to round up deserters. In Spain a force of foot and mounted Gendarmes was raised - nicknamed the "Little Gendarmerie" - to combat the swarming local *guerrilleros* who plagued the French lines of supply and communications. These were initially deployed in 20 mixed squadrons of horse and foot based in a network of forts and blockhouses throughout northern Spain, but late in 1810 the mounted Gendarmes were concentrated into a single Legion based on Burgos; from this date they increasingly received the lance as their primary weapon.

The headgear was the *chapeau bras* or bicorn hat, here worn "en bataille" (crossways), with white trim and a red plume or pompon. Full dress was a cutaway *habit* similar to the Dragoon uniform, in dark blue faced with red and with blue grenades on the turnbacks, worn over a buff waistcoat and buff breeches. Gendarmes à Pied wore fringed red epaulettes, and infantry gaiters and accoutrements with buff belting; mounted Gendarmes wore this aiguilette on the left shoulder, and kneeboots. During a halt on patrol, our trooper wears here a simpler single-breasted *surtout* jacket and *pantalons à cheval* in corps colours.

Line Lancers

(**Right**) A trooper of the 1er Chevau-Légers Lanciers, c.1812, on campaign; note oat sack and hay net slung from his saddle. Feeding the horses was a constant problem for Napoleonic armies, as much of the cavalry was almost always operating far ahead of the logistical "tail" of the army. Horses being ridden daily over large distances need adequate grazing or cut fodder if they are not to lose condition and flesh within a matter of days. The tens of thousands of horses found in a large Napoleonic army consumed huge quantities daily, "eating out" wide swathes of countryside; when on the march too large a proportion of the cavalry therefore tended to be ever more widely dispersed on foraging expeditions.

On 18 June 1811 Napoleon, impressed by the performance of his Polish lancers of the Imperial Guard and the Vistula Legion, signed a decree ordering into existence the new Line Lancer regiments of the French cavalry - the Chevau-Légers Lanciers. The 1st to 6th Lancers were formed respectively from the 1st, 3rd, 8th, 9th, 10th and 29th Dragoons; and subsequently 7th and 8th Regiments were formed from the old Vistula Legion, and a 9th from the 30th Chasseurs à Cheval. Their uniform was basically similar to that of the Dragoons, with minor differences.

Although they were not fully organised by the time of the Russian campaign the Lancers - whom Napoleon had envisaged as a counter to the Russian Cossacks - acquitted themselves well at Smolensk, Borodino, Polotsk, the Berezina, and in 1813 at Dresden, Leipzig and Hanau. All six regiments fought in Belgium during the Waterloo campaign. Initially their role was conceived as performing light cavalry duties for the divisions of heavy Cuirassiers; but by 1813, their potential in the line of battle being realised, they were themselves used as part of the "mass of decision" on the battlefield.

(**Below**) At the charge a well-trained lancer could be a formidable opponent, but in the hands of a poor horseman the lance became an impediment. An inexperienced lancer could allow the lance to penetrate too deeply into an opponent's body, being dragged from the saddle when he was unable to recover the point as he rode past. "Tent-pegging" with the lance against a target on the ground is as much a matter of avoiding being knocked out by the butt end of the lance as of placing the point with precision. To learn to use the lance effectively took hours of practice; recruits began their lance drill by learning the movements on foot, with their left hand positioned as if holding the reins. The movements were broken down into thrusts, parries and cuts. When a cycle of movements was completed the lancer reverted to the guard position with the reins held short in the left hand and the lance held at the point of balance in the right, the thumb on top and the fingers around the shaft; the forearm supported the shaft and held it in place two inches below the breast. Against a mounted enemy the lancer was to give point at the height of the horse's ears; when his target was on foot the lance was to be pointed at the height of the horse's nostrils.

The Lancer regiments wore a green habit-veste with pointed cuffs and plastron lapels, the six regiments being distinguished by facing colours on collar, cuffs, lapels and turnbacks: scarlet, orange, pink, crimson, sky blue and madder red respectively for the 1st to 6th Regiments, all of which wore brass buttons and yellow lace and were supposed to wear green Imperial eagle badges on the jacket turnbacks. Their headgear was a modification of the Dragoon helmet with an added leather peak at the rear, and a fur roach on the crest in place of the Dragoons' falling horsehair mane.

(**Above & above right**) Lancers could be employed as light cavalry to provide outposts. These consisted of four parts: nearest the enemy was the vedette of one or two men, who remained constantly mounted. Further back was the "small post" of about ten men and an NCO, whose horses were kept bridled, to skirmish in support of the vedettes if the enemy approached. The "grand guard", of company or squadron strength and providing the personnel for the smaller forward outposts in rotation, stayed further back; half could unbridle at any time. Piquets, the final link in the chain to the main body, were allowed to light fires and to shelter in available buildings, half their horses being harnessed at any one time.

(**Right**) Lancers were trained to think of themselves as the centre of a circle, and able to thrust in any direction. This trooper practises making a full circular motion from left to right rear.

Cuirassiers

From the original corps of heavy "battle cavalry" Napoleon had created, by the end of 1803, a force of 12 armoured Cuirassier regiments and two of Carabiniers (who received the cuirass in 1809). These troopers - helmeted and armoured front and back, armed with a heavy straight sabre, pistols and, from 1812, a carbine - provided the cavalry "mass of decision". Their task was to deliver decisive charges on the field of battle, in divisional strength. Their way prepared by artillery and infantry fire to weaken and demoralise the enemy battle line, they would smash into it with irresistible weight, rupturing its formations and turning an ordered line into a disordered mob on the brink of panic flight.

Each regiment theoretically consisted of four squadrons (five, from March 1807), each of two companies, each of two troops. The establishment of each regiment's command and specialist staff was 21 officers, NCOs and tradesmen; each company supposedly had three officers, 14 NCOs, a trumpeter and 82 troopers. Thus the theoretical strength of a four-squadron regiment in 1805 was 37 officers and 784 NCOs and men, totalling 821 all ranks.

In practice, however, the rolls of the Reserve Cavalry Corps of the Grande Armée for that year show, for instance, that the 5th Cuirassiers had 32 officers, 468 other ranks and only 367 horses. Of the eight regiments listed none had over 32 officers, and four regiments 24 officers or less;

none had over 566 other ranks, and three less than 500; none had over 590 horses, and five less than 500. Mounts, as always, were a problem, especially since Cuirassiers required the largest and strongest horses available to carry armoured men in a knee-to-knee charge; after the victories over Austria and Prussia in 1805-6 the French took every opportunity to acquire some of their better horseflesh.

(Below) Officer, eagle-bearer and trooper of the reconstructed 5th Cuirassiers on the clifftops at Boulogne. In 1803 the camps around this Channel port had been the assembly point for the160,000-strong Army of England in preparation for the planned invasion. There, under the command of Soult and Ney, the Grande Armée was forged; and even after Nelson's victory over the French and Spanish fleets at Trafalgar in 1805 finally put paid to any hope of invading England the long months of gruelling training were not wasted - they were to pay dividends in battle against the Austrians and Russians in the campaigns of Ulm and Austerlitz.

(Right) The 1804 pattern standard was carried on a blue staff about two metres long. When Napoleon first presented the eagles to his battalions and squadrons on the Champ de Mars, on a dull, windswept day in December 1804, he stirred the hearts of his men by declaring: "Soldiers, here are your colours! These eagles will always be your rallying point. They will fly wherever your Emperor deems necessary for the defence of the throne and his people. Do you swear to lay down your lives in their defence, and by your courage to keep them forever on the road to victory?" "We swear it!" crashed out the reply, as the eagles were raised high in salute.

(Above & above right) 5th Cuirassiers officer; note the more elaborate shoulder fittings (cf.page 75) and red leathers, silver lace epaulette and counter epaulette, and full dress helmet plume - an officer's best plume could cost up to 100 francs, while a common soldier's cost about 3 francs, a typical example of the high cost of all officers' personally purchased, high quality dress and accoutrements. Note the straight officer's sabre carried throughout the period, although this hilt was also sometimes fitted to a slightly curved "Montmorency" blade.
Col.de Gonneville described one Sous-Lt.Marulaz of the 6th Cuirassiers: "He was 40 years old, and had no fortune but his sword; he was a strict soldier, performing his duties with scrupulous exactness, seldom smiled and never laughed...a specimen of a rare species."

(Right) 5th Cuirassiers officer and troopers. The white-trimmed red *fraise* lining which showed around the edges of the cuirass was common to all regiments, as were the troopers' fringed scarlet epaulettes.

Brigadier of the 5th in full dress uniform; the white diagonal stripes above his cuff flaps mark corporal's rank - all Cuirassier regiments wore white/silver lace and buttons. The type of cuirass used from 1802 came to a bluntly angled point at the central bottom edge; later patterns which began to appear from c.1807 had this more rounded shape. Helmets - like all such items - differed in small details, but all had an iron skull with a black fur "turban", a brass alloy crest displaying a black horsehair tuft and mane, a brass-bound leather peak and brass chinscales fastened by a *rosace* embossed with a star.

The dark blue tunic developed during the Empire from a long-tailed *habit-surtout* via intermediate patterns to a short-tailed *habit-veste* in c.1812. Regimental facing colours also changed during the period, the 5th wearing scarlet cuffs and turnbacks until c.1810, and *aurore* (peach) thereafter on the cuffs only, other areas being blue piped with facing colour. Full dress breeches were of chamois-coloured sheep or deer leather, worn with white boot-hose and heavy black boots.

(Left) A Cuirassier officer cools his horse in the sea at Boulogne; officers' saddle covers were of black fleece. Without his cuirass it is possible to see the single-breasted habit-veste coat of this branch, which was cut high at the front and worn over a white waistcoat. In such a scene it would perhaps be more usual to see the expensive deerhide breeches covered with overalls, or replaced by the dark blue cloth breeches commonly worn for field service.

(Right) Cuirassiers advance on the field of battle. For the modern re-enactor, even if an experienced horseman, learning to mount, ride and dismount in the encumbering armour and kit of a Napoleonic heavy trooper takes time and application. The author has on several occasions seen riders flipped onto the ground like turned turtles when the bottom edge of the cuirass caught on the saddle during dismounting; and a sabre hanging at the length of its slings is a snare lying constantly in wait for unwary spurred boots.

The historical 5th Cuirassiers served in all the great campaigns of Napoleon's armies: they were at Austerlitz in 1805, at Jena in 1806, and at Eylau in 1807. The 1st Squadron was detached in 1808 and sent to fight in Spain as part of the composite 1st Provisional Heavy Cavalry Regiment. In 1809 the 5th were at Eckmuehl, Ratisbonne, Aspern-Essling and Wagram. They fought at Borodino and Winkovo in 1812, and at Leipzig and Hanau in 1813. The campaign of France in 1814 found them at Montmirail, Bar-sur-Aube, Troyes, Nogent and Saint-Dizier; and in June 1815 they followed their Emperor to Ligny and Waterloo.

(Right) The horses for the heavy Cuirassier and Carabinier regiments were supposed to measure a minimum of 155cm and a maximum of 160cm from the withers (shoulder), and to be between five and eight years of age. Under campaign conditions these ideal standards were often eroded. The men themselves were to be at least 177.8cm tall for the Carabiniers and 172.8 for the Cuirassiers (roughly 5ft 10ins and 5ft 8ins respectively).

(**Above**) An officer of the 14th Cuirassiers (centre) wearing a long-tailed habit, complete with lapels in facing colour, seen with a trooper and a sergeant in stable dress. The 14th, raised in 1810 from the Dutch 2nd Cuirassiers, wore facings of *lie de vin* - "wine dregs". Note the two different ways of wearing the bonnet de police - with the "flame" tucked in or hanging free.

(**Right**) Cuirassier helmet bearing the evidence of a collision with a British heavy dragoon's sabre; fortunately in this instance nobody was hurt, but extreme care must be taken at all times during re-enactment combat displays, which are "choreographed" beforehand in some detail.

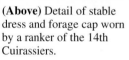

(Above) Detail of stable dress and forage cap worn by a ranker of the 14th Cuirassiers.

(Above right) 14th Cuirassiers officer and sergeant in everyday service dress around the barracks, both wearing the black felt bicorn hat. The officer wears the early style habit with cutaway front and faced lapels, and blue cloth breeches. The sergeant wears an habit-surtout, and riding overalls in drab grey; his epaulettes of rank are in mixed scarlet and silver. Note the grenade badge on the belt plate, and the difference between the sabre hilts.

(Right) Cuirassiers' cloaks developed from the sleeveless, caped patterns shown here to the sleeved manteau-capote illustrated on pages 8 & 33. The trooper's manteau was made from a thread known as *piqué de bleu* - a white and blue mix which gave this light grey effect - which was specially produced by Ian Smith for the reconstruction; Ian's wife Tass hand-tailored the 14th Cuirassier habits.

(**Above & opposite**) Rear and front views of a corporal trumpeter, an officer and a maréchal-des-logis of the 14th Cuirassiers in field dress and armour. After the 1812 regulations musicians of all Line regiments of horse and foot were supposed to wear dark green "Imperial livery", in an attempt to impose some order on the flamboyant chaos previously created by the tradition of musicians wearing reversed colours. (See page 87 for details of these late pattern helmets.)

(Right) The Imperial livery was lavishly decorated with yellow-on-green or green-on-yellow lace, with alternating Imperial eagles and Ns, and dividing lines of black and red thread; it was produced in both horizontal and vertical formats for use on various parts of the tunic. White helmet plumes and manes and white epaulettes were also worn as trumpeters' distinctions.

(Left) Trumpeters rode greys when they could be obtained; in the early years a whole troop might be mounted on greys if there was a surplus of this colour, although late in the Empire trumpeters no doubt took whatever mounts they could get. As a further immediate identification trumpeters used black saddle covers instead of white. The shabraque has the Cuirassiers' white grenade insignia, and the portmanteau is the heavy cavalry type of rectangular section.

(Below) Close-up of the saddle furniture of a 14th Cuirassiers sergeant; note also the grey *surculottes* with wooden buttons.

(Right) The maréchal-des-logis in battle; note the plaited helmet *criniére,* the thick fur turban, and the lentil-shaped pompon replacing the full dress plume. Exertion under the summer sun while wearing thick wool uniforms and iron armour is exhausting, and dehydration can be a major problem even during re-enactments. After this particular event it was found that sweat stains were hard to clean off the armour; any trace of damp on polished iron turns into a rust blister in a few hours, and sweat has a particularly corrosive effect.

(Opposite top) Some of the cuirasses used by re-enactors are originals painstakingly restored by Ian Smith and Anthony Perkins; others are reconstructions. Compare the slight variations between these pieces, particularly at the bottom edge of the breast plate.

(Far left & left) Splendid reconstructions, by Ian Smith and Paul Ellis, of an officer's cuirass and late pattern "Minerva" helmet. Note the detail of the handsome cuirass shoulder fastenings, with lion masks echoing those on the helmet chinscale bosses; and the fine silver-laced lining. The horsehair mane emerges from slots in the rear part of the crest *(cimier),* which has an enclosed top to prevent rain rotting the horsehair at the point of attachment.

(Above & above right) From c.1808 it became the fashion for officers to purchase helmets of a more pronounced pseudo-Classical shape, *"a la Minerve",* with the skull taller and more backswept, giving the front profile of skull and peak a more nearly continuous line, and the crest inclining more sharply forward; note also the fur turban carried forward over the peak. On the front of the crest an embossed Medusa mask surmounts a silver plaque bearing the regimental number.

(Right) Under the heavy fur turban this sergeant of the 14th wears the plainer model of trooper's helmet, as introduced in an effort to standardise the previously varying examples from c.1811 - compare with pages 75-77. Unsurprisingly, the opportunity was also taken to economise by using inferior materials, and disgusted Cuirassiers kept the older pieces whenever they could.

(Right) Silver embroidered grenade decorations applied to the tail turnbacks of the 14th Cuirassier officer's coat.

(Below) Reconstructed Cuirassier curb bit, by Paul Ellis of Claverdon, Warwick, from originals in the Musée de l'Armée and Musée de l'Emperi. Note the regimentally numbered bosses attached to the cheek pieces.

(Right) An *aide-de-camp* delivers a message to a Cuirassier officer. A century before radio communication, the only means of exercising command or gathering progress reports was by word of mouth or hand-written message carried by one of the suite of keen and well-mounted young officers who were attached to every general's staff.

(**Above & right**) A good deal of latitude was tolerated in the dress of aides; this officer of the early Empire period wears a light cavalry dolman and flamboyantly embroidered breeches, with the large bicorn which was the most common headgear for officers of all Napoleonic armies before about 1812, and for many thereafter. The red and gold brassard is the badge of his appointment; these echoed in miniature the sashes worn by the different ranks of formation commanders, and thus were white and gold for ADCs to a *Maréchal de l'Empire,* red and gold for those serving a *Général de Division,* and sky blue and gold for the aides to a *Général de Brigade.*

The Warrior at Rest

(Right) A Cuirassier trumpeter, wearing the reversed colours typical of the pre-1812 period, catches up on his correspondence - or perhaps upon the diary which may form the basis of his memoirs?

(Below) This Cuirassier was found lying fast asleep outside his tent after a re-enactment battle at Boulogne. "Living history" can be absolutely exhausting, especially in hot weather, and frequent gulps from a water canteen are important to avoid dehydration. For the cavalry trooper there are many camp chores which cannot be neglected even when off duty, given the high level of care required by their horses and tack.

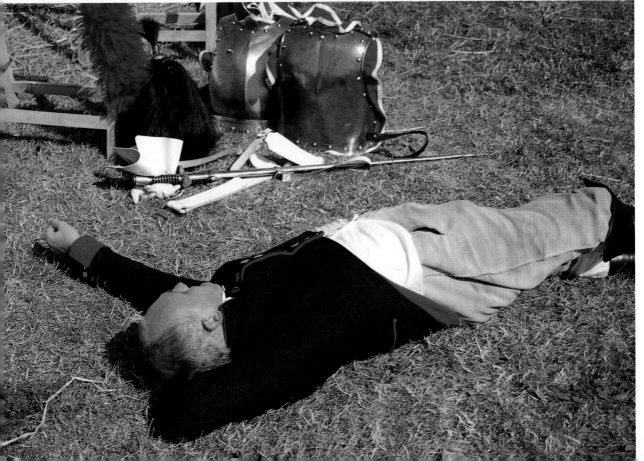

In pre-modern armies the supplies and services provided for the soldiers by the central logistic administration were minimal. A soldier on campaign could look to the army to provide him with a uniform, shoes, and a coat and/ or a blanket, in addition to his weapons and ammunition. Tents for the rank and file were hardly ever provided, and shelter in the field was a matter of bivouacs rigged up with blankets and branches.

Some kind of daily food ration was the norm - if he was lucky, and if the commissariat was working smoothly; but this might well be limited to bread or biscuit, and in French armies it was not unusual for meat and greenstuff to be left up to the ingenuity, and ruthlessness, of pillagers "living off the country". French military medical services were actually quite advanced by the grim standards of the day, but were still elementary, being limited to the crudest care of traumatic injury after battle, and were overwhelmed by the numbers of casualties after all major actions.

For many necessities, including the nursing of invalids through minor injury and mundane illness, and for all the small comforts of daily life - laundry, sewing, tobacco, alcohol and other canteen goods, additional food, etc. - the soldiers therefore had to rely on female camp-followers. Napoleonic armies were always followed by an unofficial but tolerated "tail" of civilians, many of them women, who catered to the needs of the troops, and without whom the armies could not have functioned. Sharing the

hardship and danger of campaign life, individual traders of every sort peddled their wares and services; and among them the *cantiniéres* or *vivandiéres* who attached themselves to French units enjoyed a superior and semi-official status. Often married to an NCO, and tricked out in some approximation of regimental costume, these enterprising and resourceful women did a brisk trade whenever they arrived in camp with their cart or pack-panniers to offer brandy, wine, tobacco and fresh food - especially in cavalry camps, which were often the furthest from the baggage train.

These photographs show two of the charming *vivandiéres* who accompanied the cavalry to the re-enactment camp at Boulogne to conduct their business "across the saddle".

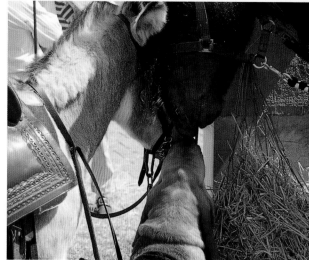

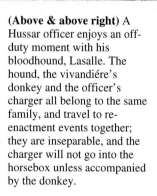

(Above & above right) A Hussar officer enjoys an off-duty moment with his bloodhound, Lasalle. The hound, the vivandiére's donkey and the officer's charger all belong to the same family, and travel to re-enactment events together; they are inseparable, and the charger will not go into the horsebox unless accompanied by the donkey.

(Right) More than usually succulent rations are enthusiastically tested for tenderness by a Horse Artillery sergeant in the cavalry bivouac at Montmirail.

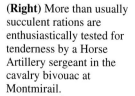

(Left & below)

In re-enactment camps, as in Napoleonic times, the soldiers are sometimes lucky enough to have the company of their womenfolk to do the cooking - a boon for troopers who have their horses to care for when they come out of the line. Preparing and cooking food for large numbers using only open fires and period utensils is an acquired skill - and those who acquire it are much prized by groups re-enacting all historical periods. At least these hardy campaigners encamped at Boulogne have the advantage of fine weather; trying to keep a recreated unit fed on a muddy campsite in prolonged rain is a task which brings a special understanding of the Napoleonic soldier's lot.